Incredibly Disgusting Drugs ™

Tobacco

Jason Porterfield

rosen publishing's

rosen central®

New York

Published in 2008 by The Rosen Publishing Group, Inc.
29 East 21st Street, New York, NY 10010

Copyright © 2008 by The Rosen Publishing Group, Inc.

First Edition

Library of Congress Cataloging-in-Publication Data

Porterfield, Jason.
Tobacco / Jason Porterfield.
      p.cm.—(Incredibly disgusting drugs)
Includes bibliographical references.
ISBN-13: 978-1-4042-1378-4 (lib. bdg.)
1. Tobacco use. 2. Smoking. 3. Tobacco—Physiological effect. I. Title.
HV5735.P67 2008
362.29'6—dc22

                                                                2007029522

Manufactured in the United States of America

Contents

Introduction

"I can quit any time" is a phrase often spoken by steady tobacco users. They may not believe that their smoking or chewing habit is an addiction, as real and deadly as any other chemical dependency. The truth is that all tobacco products contain an addictive chemical called nicotine. Once the body develops a tolerance for nicotine, it's very difficult to stop using tobacco.

Nicotine is one of the most addictive chemicals on Earth, as habit-forming as so-called hard drugs like cocaine. A drug is any substance that alters the way a person's body functions, an effect that nicotine definitely has on tobacco users. Tobacco is every bit as deadly as harder drugs, though the damage it causes—such as heart disease and cancer—might not be apparent for years.

Even when tobacco users recognize that they have an addiction, it can be very hard for them to stop. They may offer any number of excuses, ranging from feeling bored when they're not smoking to being afraid that they'll gain weight when they quit. They may feel that they need tobacco to concentrate and handle stress, or that they've already waited too long to quit.

It's actually never too late to quit. According to Edwin Fisher's *7 Steps to a Smoke-Free Life*—a book endorsed by the American Lung Association—the body begins to repair itself almost immediately after your last cigarette. Within twenty minutes, your blood pressure and pulse rate drop back to normal levels. Eight hours after the last cigarette, oxygen and carbon monoxide levels in the blood return to normal. Within forty-eight hours, the chance of having a heart attack goes down and your senses of smell and taste increase.

The improvements continue over time so that within nine months your circulation and lung functions improve, while side effects like coughing and shortness of breath decrease. By the time you celebrate your first tobacco-free year, your chances of getting coronary heart disease will be less than half that when you were smoking.

1

Who Uses Tobacco?

People have used tobacco for thousands of years. They've smoked it, snorted it, chewed it, and even drank its juice. Native Americans used tobacco in ceremonies and rituals. In some cases, healers used the plant that tobacco comes from as medicine.

European colonists picked up the tobacco habit, and smoking became popular in European cities like London. Demand grew quickly. At the same time, England's new colony in Virginia was on the brink of failure. When the English settler John Rolfe landed in Virginia in 1609, he found that tobacco grew well in the region.

Rolfe's discovery turned tobacco into a cash crop for England and gave colonists a reason to expand their territory at the expense of the Native Americans already living there. Within ten years, the colony was producing so much tobacco that the colonists couldn't tend it by themselves. Their solution was to bring the first African slaves to the colony in 1619.

Farmers in the Virginia colonies devoted most of their land and energy to growing tobacco, rather than raising edible crops. Here, farm workers harvest tobacco leaves on an early plantation.

England's hunger for tobacco therefore began two of America's most disgraceful episodes: the forced removal of Native Americans from lands they had occupied for centuries and a slave trade that lasted until the end of the American Civil War (1861–1865). Even after tobacco stopped being the most valued product exported from the former colonies, its use continued and widened. Even as late as 1883, one-third of the federal government's tax revenues came from tobacco taxes.

Cigarettes, the most widely used tobacco product, were introduced in the mid-1800s and became incredibly popular. By the 1940s, however, people began to link cigarette smoking with cancer and lung damage. Tobacco companies introduced filters to the cigarettes they sold, claiming that they made cigarettes safer. They also began covering up evidence linking cigarettes to a wide range of diseases, including emphysema, heart disease, and lung cancer.

Changing Attitudes

In 1966, nearly 43 percent of Americans smoked. It was legal to smoke inside many public spaces, including department stores and movie theaters, and on airplanes. Athletes, movie stars, and politicians frequently were shown smoking. Celebrities often endorsed certain cigarette brands. Cigarette companies used marketing symbols like the Marlboro Man to sell their products, gearing their ads to appeal to young people and to make smoking seem cool.

Nearly half a century later, however, pressure from health experts and groups like the American Lung Association has brought about laws to keep people under eighteen from buying tobacco products. Other laws make it illegal to market tobacco products to young people. Tobacco companies are also required to put labels on tobacco products that warn users of the health consequences of smoking. The public backlash against tobacco has even caused many sporting events to drop tobacco companies as sponsors.

Movie icon Audrey Hepburn smoked throughout her role as the glamorous and carefree Holly Golightly in the 1961 movie *Breakfast at Tiffany's.*

In recent years, states and individuals began suing tobacco companies, charging that they had misled the public about the dangers of cigarettes. States have raised cigarette taxes, making a product that was once very inexpensive much more costly in hopes of getting people to think twice about buying cigarettes.

Who Uses Tobacco

While there aren't nearly as many smokers today as there were in 1966, more than forty million Americans still smoke, despite the known health risks and efforts to restrict public smoking. According to the National Youth Tobacco Survey, one in eight middle school students admitted to using some form of tobacco. One-third of high school seniors admit to having used some form of tobacco in the last thirty days, while about 25 percent claim to be active smokers.

While smoking in general has declined, it has increased among young women. At least twenty-two million smokers are women. The American Cancer Society reports that 60,000 women die of lung cancer every year, quadruple the number from 1960.

Tobacco's Cost

The World Health Organization estimates that in developed countries, about 26 percent of male deaths and 9 percent of female deaths can be linked to smoking. In the United States, about 438,000 people, enough to fill eight baseball stadiums, die each year as a result of smoking. That number breaks down to around 1,205 deaths a day. More people die each year as a result of tobacco use than from motor vehicle accidents, murders, suicides, illegal drug use, and alcohol combined.

The list of diseases and health problems linked with tobacco use is long and shocking. The main risks are lung diseases, heart and cardio-vascular problems, and cancer. Smokers have a 25 percent chance of developing an incurable condition called chronic obstructive pulmonary disease, which reduces smokers' ability to breathe properly and makes them susceptible to respiratory diseases like bronchitis and emphysema. Smokers are also two to four times more likely to develop heart disease than nonsmokers and are twice as likely to suffer from a stroke or a heart attack.

Smoking causes about 90 percent of lung cancer deaths. The chances that a smoker will develop lung cancer are between twelve and twenty-two

The National Cancer Institute says secondhand smoke contains more than fifty harmful chemicals. There is no safe level of secondhand smoke.

times higher than for a nonsmoker. The likelihood of other kinds of cancer also increases with tobacco use. Smoking causes four out of every five cases of esophageal cancer cases and a third of pancreatic cancer deaths, and it has been linked to numerous other cancers. In some cases, it can take up to twenty years for cancer to develop. The longer a person smokes, the greater the risk becomes. On average, smoking takes about seven years off a person's lifespan.

Evidence that secondhand smoke can be harmful to people who are constantly exposed to it—such as restaurant workers or entertainers who perform in smoky clubs—has played a major role in bringing about some indoor smoking bans. About 38,000 Americans die each year as a result of secondhand smoke.

Killed by Tobacco

Actors Humphrey Bogart and John Wayne were longtime smokers and eventual cancer victims who helped glamorize tobacco in their movies. U.S. president Ulysses S. Grant smoked cigars until dying of throat cancer. News anchor Peter Jennings, former Texas governor Ann Richards, and ex-Beatles member George Harrison are just a few of the famous people who have died from smoking in recent years.

Chewing tobacco and snuff have long been considered less socially acceptable than cigarettes because users have to spit frequently to avoid swallowing tobacco juice. Prior to the introduction of cigarettes in the nineteenth century, public buildings provided containers called spittoons for chewers to use to get rid of their tobacco juice. Cigars and pipes, which have a stronger odor than cigarettes, were less commonly used in public.

Today, many people are aware that cigarettes are harmful. Since cigar and pipe smoke isn't inhaled as deeply as cigarette smoke, cigars and pipes are often used as substitutes for cigarettes, even though they also cause cancer and other health problems.

The tobacco industry has a long history of cutting deals with the federal government in order to keep making a profit. In the 1960s, tobacco

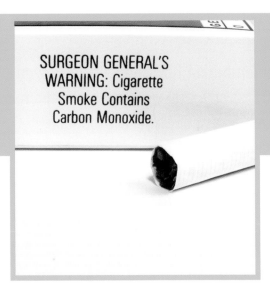

SURGEON GENERAL'S WARNING: Cigarette Smoke Contains Carbon Monoxide.

The first warning label to appear on cigarette packages read, "Cigarette smoking may be hazardous to your health." Today, the label is much more specific about the health risks of smoking.

companies voluntarily agreed to stop advertising their products on television when children were likely to be watching, prior to a 1971 ban on television ads. Later deals led to companies putting warning labels on packs and voluntary restrictions on selling cigarettes near schools.

However, the industry wasn't doing this for the public good. Many television shows and movies showed glamorous actors and actresses smoking. Smoking was rarely seen in a negative light, with directors neglecting to show their smoking characters coughing up mucus or suffering from emphysema. Even cartoon characters smoked. During baseball games, respected athletes were often seen chewing tobacco, even saying that it helped them concentrate. This essentially amounted to free advertising for the companies, as people took up smoking or chewing to appear more like their heroes. Today, it has become harder to find smoking characters on television shows, though movies continue to romanticize smoking.

The Lure of Tobacco

Tobacco users often have trouble remembering how they started, even if they can easily recall how sick their first cigarette or chew made them. They also may not remember when they first noticed yellow tobacco stains on their fingers, or when their teeth started turning brown from chewing. If they've been smoking for a long time, they may not even remember what it feels like to breathe with undamaged lungs.

People start using tobacco for any number of reasons, none of them good. They might see it as a way to pass the time at a boring job or to relieve stress, even though nicotine acts as a stimulant. Many teens start because they see smoking as a way to look cool and rebellious or because their friends smoke. They might get a thrill just from acquiring cigarettes and feeling as though they're getting away with something. Smokeless tobacco users begin for many of the same reasons, in the false belief that snuff and chewing tobacco are safer than cigarettes, cigars, or pipes. They may even be former smokers who started using smokeless tobacco as a substitute for cigarettes.

2

Just
the Facts

Many smokers start slowly, having only a few cigarettes a week. As they build a tolerance to the chemicals and additives found in tobacco, they smoke more heavily. Before too long, they've developed an addiction to nicotine. Smokers may claim to enjoy a buzz that comes with their first cigarette of the day, as their bodies absorb the nicotine that they've been craving. As they take that first puff, they begin introducing thousands of harmful chemicals into their bodies.

Tobacco's Deadly Forms

Farmers all over the world grow tobacco, a toxic plant distantly related to potatoes and the poisonous deadly nightshade. At the end of the season, tobacco farmers harvest the leaves and cure them, drying them out so that they can be turned into tobacco products. Historically, the leaves were simply hung up and allowed to dry out. Today, there are several ways to cure tobacco.

Newer methods of curing make tobacco stronger, more addictive, and more deadly. Once the tobacco is cured, farmers sell it to tobacco companies, who turn it into cigarettes, cigars, snuff, and chewing tobacco. Tobacco processors also use tobacco to make poisons such as weed killer.

Tobacco products take many forms, and all of them are dangerous. Pipe smoking was once the most common way to take tobacco. During the 1700s, people started to use tobacco as a finely ground powder called snuff, which they snorted up their noses. Snuff was very popular with the wealthy, even though it made users sneeze.

In past years, baseball players like outfielder Lenny Dykstra often chewed tobacco on the field. Today's players are more aware of the health risks of smokeless tobacco and often avoid it.

Today, most tobacco users either smoke it in the form of cigarettes or cigars, or they chew it as chewing tobacco or snuff. Chewing tobacco users stuff wads of dried and processed tobacco leaves into their mouths and chew them to extract the tobacco juice. The juice stains their teeth brown, and they have to spit constantly to get rid of it. Chewing tobacco burns and numbs the mouth, and it often makes first-time users sick.

Snuff, or "dip," is much more finely ground tobacco. It comes in wet or dry varieties. Dry snuff is snorted. Wet snuff is usually taken as a pinch placed between the user's gum line and lower lip. Dark and pre-moistened, it looks a lot like potting soil.

Tobacco companies add flavoring ingredients to wet snuff and chewing tobacco to make it easier to take. Though the flavoring ingredients—such as mint—may mask the taste of cured and processed tobacco, they can't cover up the hazards of smokeless tobacco.

Inside the Cigarette

Every part of a cigarette, from the tobacco inside to the filter, contains poisonous chemicals. Tobacco companies add more than 4,000 chemicals to cigarettes, from the dye used to print the brand's logo to chemicals designed to keep the filter's paper covering from sticking to the smoker's lips. The radioactive elements radium and polonium occur naturally in tobacco leaves. Farmers also spray their plants with fertilizers, pesticides, and fungicides as they grow. All of those things remain in the tobacco after it is cured and processed. As the tobacco is processed, companies add chemicals and flavorings like licorice to mask its bitter taste.

When a person smokes a filtered cigarette, a yellow tar stain shows up at the end of the filter. Despite the filter, tar still enters the lungs.

The white paper cylinder that holds the tobacco is full of chemicals designed to make it look whiter and burn evenly. The paper is bleached and dyed to make it appear bright white. Companies also treat cigarette paper with chemicals found in rocket fuel to keep them from burning out. As a consequence, a cigarette will smolder steadily until it reaches the filter. This leads to thousands of fires every year, as smokers either throw away still-burning cigarette butts or put them down and forget about them.

As a cigarette burns, it releases nicotine through a complex chemical compound commonly called tar. Filters were first introduced to block some of this unhealthy tar, but they actually do very little to stop it. Smokers simply have to take longer and deeper drags from their cigarettes to get the chemicals they crave. In fact, filters themselves contain chemicals that increase the speed at which nicotine reaches the brain. The tobacco industry spent years and millions of dollars to find a way to deliver nicotine through the filter. One of the chemicals they use is ammonia, commonly found in bathroom cleaning products. Most smokers probably don't realize

The Myth of Light Cigarettes

Many tobacco companies sell "light" versions of their more famous brands, claiming that they filter out more tar and are therefore safer. Because of the lower tar content, people who smoke these brands actually inhale more deeply and keep the smoke in their lungs longer than other smokers, making them just as unhealthy as regular cigarettes.

that their cigarettes contain ammonia, the same chemical they use to clean their toilets.

Regulating Tobacco

For years, tobacco companies made enormous profits while the government did little to regulate tobacco use. Companies such as Brown & Williamson, Phillip Morris, and R. J. Reynolds took baby steps to appease antismoking groups while continuing their research on how to make cigarettes more addictive. They even made public contributions to charities—including cancer research centers—to appear generous and civic-minded. Other contributions went to politicians with the power to block any moves to regulate tobacco.

In 1999, a jury found that the tobacco industry was liable for causing illnesses such as cancer and for hiding evidence about tobacco's dangers. Guillermo Saa (*center*) was the lead plaintiff in the case.

The 1990s, however, saw a shift in the relationship between the government and the tobacco companies. In 1994, Mississippi became the first state to sue the tobacco companies to recover the cost of medical care for millions of ailing smokers. In 1998, tobacco companies agreed to a multibillion-dollar settlement with forty-six U.S. states.

Today, the legal age for buying cigarettes in the United States is eighteen. In many states, underage smokers can be fined for buying, possessing, or using tobacco products. People of legal age who purchase tobacco products for minors can be punished with fines, as can cashiers who sell tobacco products to underage people. If someone buying tobacco products looks younger than twenty-seven, the cashier is required to ask for identification to verify that person's age. Police officers also have the power to fine people who violate public smoking bans.

Even after the lawsuits and settlements, as well as recent efforts by cities and towns to ban public smoking, the tobacco industry continues to make money and influence politicians through political contributions. While they still sell millions of packs of cigarettes to U.S. customers, they have recently begun focusing their marketing efforts on other countries, where laws are less restrictive.

3
Tobacco
and Your
Body

For decades, Marlboro cigarettes used the Marlboro Man to advertise its product. The Marlboro Man was a rugged cowboy, independent and prepared to master any situation. With the Marlboro Man representing its brand, Marlboro cigarettes became the first choice for many young smokers.

Though he appeared able to handle anything, the good-looking and physically fit Marlboro Man couldn't be a less representative model for tobacco's effects on health and appearance. The real effects of tobacco are much uglier. Tobacco companies probably wouldn't sell as many cigarettes if they showed their smokers pulling an oxygen tank behind them or disfigured by a tracheotomy. They don't really want people to think about how decades of smoking will leave their skin leathery and wrinkled. They especially don't want to bother potential customers with boring statistics about how much smoking is likely to reduce their lifespan.

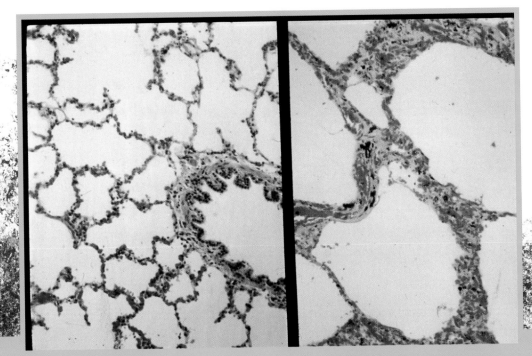

Healthy lung tissue *(left)* contains small air sacs called alveoli. In the lung tissue of a patient with emphysema *(right)*, the walls of the alveoli have deteriorated, creating much larger air spaces.

And the suffering experienced by smokers who develop deadly health conditions due to tobacco use? That definitely wouldn't be good advertising.

The Immediate Effects

When a smoker takes a drag of a cigarette, the smoke moves into the airways of the lungs and tiny air sacs called alveoli. From there, nicotine and numerous other toxic chemicals are absorbed into the blood.

Eventually, these substances have to leave the body. Thus, the kidneys, liver, gastrointestinal tract, and other areas of the body are exposed to—and potentially damaged by—the chemicals introduced into the body in the form of tobacco smoke. This is why smoking is called a "multisystem" cause of disease.

A person's first cigarette is generally a revolting experience. It burns the mouth and tastes vile, and it causes immediate retching. Even worse are the side effects of nicotine. Nicotine is a deadly poison, though each cigarette contains only a small amount. A dose of nicotine causes the heart to beat more quickly, blood pressure to rise, and metabolism to increase. Someone trying nicotine for the first time will feel dizziness, a headache, and nausea.

So why do smokers claim that cigarettes calm the nerves, relieve stress, and help them feel relaxed and alert? Over time, they develop a tolerance to nicotine. It takes a larger amount to achieve the same effect.

As tobacco's deadly side effects have been scientifically proven and become well known to the public, tobacco companies have increased promotion of other tobacco products. Some people who are savvy about tobacco risks may be tempted by cigars or smokeless tobacco, thinking that they're not as dangerous. That's not the case—there's no safe alternative to cigarettes. Although the specific toxins and health risks may vary from one type of tobacco product to another, they all contain carcinogens, or cancer-causing chemicals, and lead to nasty side effects.

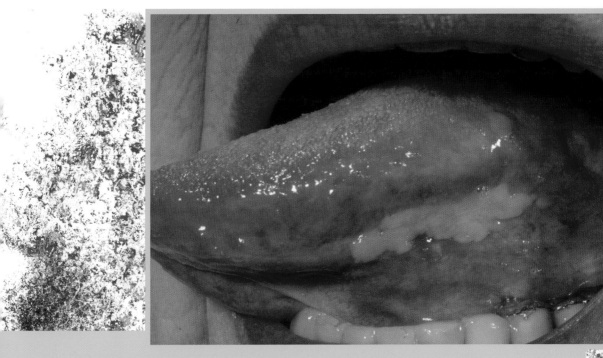

Smokeless tobacco irritates the tongue, cheek, and gums. Prolonged use can cause people to develop thick, white patches called leukoplakia, a condition that can lead to cancer.

Cigar smokers may argue that they smoke only a few cigars a day, so they are not as dangerous. Perhaps they never noticed that a single cigar can contain as much tobacco as an entire pack of cigarettes. They are higher in tar and in nicotine. Also, cigar smokers don't inhale as deeply, so they ingest nicotine differently. Cigar smoke is more alkaline than cigarette smoke, which means that it passes through the membranes of the mouth more easily. There's no less of a risk of developing cancer for cigar smokers.

When someone uses smokeless tobacco, nicotine and other toxins are absorbed through the membranes of the mouth over a much longer period of time than when smoked. Since smokeless tobacco doesn't enter the lungs, it must be safer than cigarettes, right? No—though it doesn't cause lung cancer or emphysema, it is responsible for a variety of other medical conditions. Spitting is by no means the worst side effect. Like any other form of tobacco, it contains nicotine and is highly addictive. White patches called leukoplakia can develop into oral cancer; smokeless tobacco may also cause cancer of the larynx, lip, cheek, tongue, esophagus, stomach, or bladder. Like cigarettes, it's linked to heart disease. It also causes gum problems, awful breath, damage to the jawbone, and rotten and yellowed teeth.

Consequences of Continued Use

It doesn't take long for tobacco use to impact a smoker's health. Even an occasional cigarette will affect the lungs. Smoke burns the cilia—tiny hairs in the air passages—or causes them to become coated in mucus. Tar starts to build up. The alveoli can get clogged. Carbon monoxide reduces oxygen levels in the blood. All of these factors add up to wheezing, impaired lungs. Smokers are also more prone to respiratory ailments such as asthma. Shortness of breath affects athletic performance, as does the raised metabolic levels and heart rate. Although cardiovascular disease is uncommon among young adults, smokers are far more likely to be afflicted.

The cosmetic side effects of smoking aren't very attractive either. If you're repulsed by the smell of stale cigarette smoke surrounding a smoker, don't get close to his or her breath. Things just get worse the longer someone smokes. Fingers and fingernails become permanently stained. So do the teeth. Later in life, smoking contributes to gum disease such as gingivitis, the development of osteoporosis, and even hair loss. Tobacco also ages the skin prematurely—smokers tend to develop wrinkles and deep creases earlier than nonsmokers.

It's well known that tobacco numbs people's sense of taste and smell. Longtime smokers may be more likely to develop eye conditions such as damaged retinas or glaucoma. There's also a type of vision loss exclusive to tobacco users called tobacco amblyopia. Smoking even affects the voice by irritating the larynx. Taste, smell, sight (if affected by tobacco amblyopia), and speaking voice generally improve when a smoker quits.

A Deadly Habit

Every tobacco product contains dozens of carcinogens. These toxic chemicals can cause damage to a person's DNA, which leads to the production of mutated cells. These may form cancerous lumps or tumors that disrupt the normal functioning of the surrounding area. One of the deadliest killers linked to tobacco is lung cancer. Growths develop in the air passages and alveoli, then can spread throughout the lungs and invade other parts of the body. Treatments may include surgery, radiation, and chemotherapy, but fewer than 15 percent of lung cancer victims live for more than five years after diagnosis. Smoking can also cause cancer of the larynx, mouth, esophagus, pancreas, kidney, and bladder.

Lung cancer is not the only respiratory disease caused by tobacco. Smokers have an elevated risk of developing a condition labeled chronic obstructive pulmonary disease (COPD), which means that there has been irreversible damage done to the lungs. The most notorious chronic lung ailment is emphysema, caused by the destruction of the alveoli and damage to air passages. This causes lungs to lose elasticity. A person with emphysema is able to inhale but has difficulty exhaling. As a result, there's a shortage of oxygen

This cancerous lung shows the consequences of years of smoking–tumors, blackened blotches in the tissue, and visible holes. A healthy lung is smooth and light tan in color.

and excess carbon dioxide in the system. When it gets really bad, emphysema forces sufferers to rely on oxygen from a tank.

Smokers also have a greater risk of another long-term respiratory condition called chronic bronchitis. This is a painful inflammation of the lining of the airways. Excess mucus builds up and clogs the air passages. Chronic bronchitis sufferers feel as if they're choking when they try to breathe, and they develop a telltale deep cough. COPD is a long-term condition resulting from permanent damage, but smokers can slow their decline by quitting.

Longtime smokers who suffer from emphysema struggle for every breath they take. Here, a doctor observes a patient receiving oxygen-enriched air through a face mask.

Tobacco use is a major risk factor for cardiovascular disease, including heart disease, atherosclerosis (disease of the arteries), and stroke. Nicotine and many other toxic chemicals travel through the bloodstream, stressing the heart and causing damage to blood vessels. Diseases of the heart and vascular system are the leading causes of death in the United States, and tobacco use is a major contributing factor. Arterial damage also affects the function of other organs throughout the body.

Prospective parents should be aware that chemicals in tobacco can harm an unborn child. The fetus is exposed to chemicals from cigarette smoke carried through the mother's blood. The most critical period is the first three months of pregnancy, when the infant's organs and tissues are developing. Smoking during pregnancy increases the risks of miscarriage, premature delivery, or stillbirth. Infants born to a mother who smoked during pregnancy are more likely to have birth defects, low birth weight, and serious illnesses early in life. They are also at greater risk of dying of sudden infant death syndrome (SIDS). If a mother continues smoking after giving birth and breast-feeds her baby, the milk will contain chemicals from tobacco smoke.

The Risks of Secondhand Smoke

Smokers make a choice to put poisonous chemicals in their bodies. At the same time, they allow poisonous chemicals to waft in the air around them whenever they light a cigarette. This "secondhand smoke" or "passive smoking" can affect the health of anyone who breathes it. Since secondhand smoke doesn't pass through a filter, it actually contains greater amounts of some toxins.

Like directly inhaled smoke, secondhand smoke has been linked to elevated rates of lung cancer, lung conditions, and heart disease. Every year, thousands of people die from lung cancer caused by secondhand smoke. People who work in smoky environments or live with a smoker are at an increased risk to their health.

The **Marlboro Man Fights Back**

Wayne McLaren was just one of several actors who have portrayed the Marlboro Man. He became an antismoking advocate shortly after he was diagnosed with lung cancer, appearing in an antismoking commercial that showed his wasted body hooked up to tubes. McLaren died in 1992, at the age of fifty-two.

Children are especially vulnerable to the effects of secondhand smoke. Children with a parent who smokes are far more likely to suffer from respiratory illnesses such as bronchitis, pneumonia, or asthma. Secondhand smoke can also affect lung development. Legislation and voluntary bans can clear smoke out of public places, but a smoke-filled home environment will still endanger a child's health.

4
Quitting This Disgusting Drug

"Just quit." It's easy to say, but for habitual smokers, quitting can be a monumental, possibly excruciating task. They've taken a long, hard look at the health consequences. They've figured out that smelling like a walking ashtray isn't particularly cool. They don't like the idea of funneling hard-earned money directly into the tobacco industry. But still, they keep on lighting up. Nicotine addiction and entrenched habits stymie many people's plans of swearing off of tobacco. Quitting requires a firm commitment, iron resolve in times of temptation, and, all too often, the ability to reassess and try again after a relapse.

Battling Addiction

Antismoking organizations often cite that nicotine is more addictive than heroin or alcohol and that cigarettes are an ideal means of delivering nicotine quickly. When a smoker inhales, the nicotine rushes to the brain in less

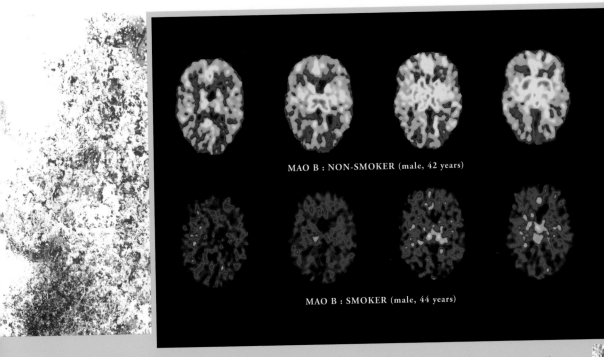

MAO B : NON-SMOKER (male, 42 years)

MAO B : SMOKER (male, 44 years)

Scans of a smoker's brain show the changes that nicotine addiction can cause. The green spots in the smoker's brain show the activated chemical receptors that cause the nicotine rush.

than ten seconds. It activates receptors in the brain, creating the rush that keeps addicts lighting up again and again. Because nicotine causes immediate changes in the brain's chemistry, a smoker's first cigarette of the day has the greatest effect. With every subsequent cigarette, the body develops a greater tolerance to nicotine. Throughout the day, addicts tend to smoke more but feel less of an effect. Overnight, the levels of nicotine in the body drop, and the cycle begins again the next day.

About ten cigarettes a day are required to satisfy a nicotine addiction. This is why many smokers trying to quit gradually have trouble cutting back to fewer than ten. A smoker's dependence on tobacco goes beyond the physical addiction to nicotine. Part of the habit is automatically reaching for a cigarette in response to certain situations. Cigarettes make an appearance after meals, when hanging out with friends, during a car trip, or before going to bed. When smokers are stressed or anxious, they light up a cigarette. When they are bored, they light up a cigarette. After the pattern is repeatedly reinforced, they automatically associate such situations with smoking.

Both the physical addiction and entrenched behavioral patterns make it hard for smokers to quit and keep their resolve. Over the short term, many smokers can't handle the physical discomfort of nicotine withdrawal. The brain adapts in response to a constant availability of nicotine. It comes to depend on nicotine for normal functioning. Withdrawal symptoms occur when the nicotine supply ceases. These may include depression, anxiety, irritability, difficulty concentrating, insomnia, low energy, headaches, digestive trouble, dizziness, increased appetite, and, of course, intense craving for cigarettes. Withdrawal begins an hour or two after the final cigarette, peaks twenty-four to forty-eight hours later, and generally tapers off over the next few weeks as the brain readjusts to a nicotine-free existence.

Even after surviving the withdrawal period, many smokers eventually relapse. Often, it's a matter of falling back into old habits. Former smokers return to cigarettes as a way to cope with stress. They give in to temptation when they're at a gathering where everyone else is smoking. For many people, the single slipup sabotages the whole effort of quitting.

Smokers, like this one, often feel the need to light up when they're in unfamiliar social settings. Satisfying their nicotine cravings may make them feel more secure.

The Benefits of Quitting

Because it's so hard to quit, most smokers have to make a firm commitment and plan out a strategy for quitting. Many smoking cessation programs recommend that the smoker make a list of the benefits of quitting. When the smoker's resolve weakens, the list will act as a reminder of the long-term reasons to resist the short-term temptation to relapse.

The most obvious reason to quit is health. Smoking—and secondhand smoke—raises a person's likelihood of eventually developing a host of excruciating medical conditions, including cancer and heart disease. There are immediate health benefits, too, such as improved taste and smell, and leaving behind a smoker's cough and shortness of breath.

The cost of smoking is another incentive for quitting. Many smokers calculate the expense of their habit and figure out things they could do with the savings. Say someone smokes twenty cigarettes every day— that's one pack. If a pack costs about $4.50, a year of smoking costs more than $1,500.

There are a variety of other reasons for quitting. Some smokers begin to resent their reliance on cigarettes and see quitting as a way to take control of their lives. Some keep their resolve by reminding themselves that they don't really want to finance the tobacco industry. Others want to set a better example for family and friends.

Personal motivations for quitting are important, too. Adults often quit before becoming a parent, for example. If you're a teen smoker, perhaps you want to quit before starting your next school year or before going off to

Many state and local governments have forced the price of cigarettes up, often well above $4, by raising cigarette taxes.

college. If you're involved in sports, maybe you want to improve your athletic performance. Perhaps your friends have encouraged you to quit in the past. This is the chance to prove to them, as well as to yourself, that you can stick to your resolve.

Methods of Quitting

Many smokers set an official "Quit Day" for breaking their habit. Beforehand, they prepare ways for coping with withdrawal and temptation. They get rid of cigarettes, matches, and ashtrays. They plan strategies for dealing with physical withdrawal symptoms and resisting the usual "triggers" to smoke. Many quitters list ways to distract themselves from smoking or reward themselves for sticking it out.

There's no single foolproof method of quitting. Some smokers join a structured smoking cessation program or follow a plan endorsed by experts. The American Lung Association, for example, has the Tobacco-Free Teens

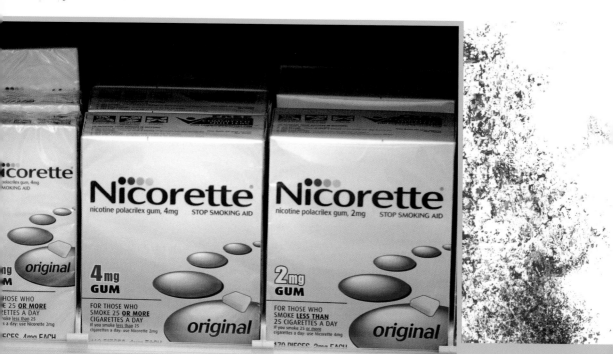

Nicotine gums such as Nicorette help smokers quit by providing them with another way of taking in nicotine. Users are supposed to gradually cut back on the amount that they chew.

program. Most programs involve the "cold turkey" approach in which smokers make a complete break with cigarettes. Some, though, succeed in quitting through the taper method, where they gradually cut back on their smoking.

Smokers often find a substitute for cigarettes when they give up smoking. Sometimes this is intentional, such as with nicotine replacement therapies or taking up a new interest for distraction. Other times, former smokers don't realize that they're compensating. One of the most notorious side effects of quitting is weight gain. Instead of reaching for a cigarette to put in their mouths, former smokers tend to grab a snack. The possibility of weight gain is heightened by the fact that a person's metabolism changes when he or she quits. Therefore, many smoking cessation plans emphasize the importance of an overall healthy lifestyle.

The most direct substitute for tobacco products is nicotine itself, usually supplied through patches, chewing gum, nasal sprays, or inhalers. These nicotine replacement therapies provide the brain with enough nicotine to forestall withdrawal symptoms and cravings. The doses are gradually reduced and finally stopped.

Other approaches involve behaviors and routines that may help people break the habit for good. Some smokers try hypnosis—a hypnotist puts them in a trance state and offers suggestions to reinforce their resolve. Others turn to alternative means such as meditation, yoga, acupuncture, herbal medicine, and aromatherapy. Many people begin an exercise regimen at the same time they swear off of smoking. Physical activity can offer an outlet during times of boredom or stress when a smoker might otherwise have grabbed a cigarette. Stretching, taking a walk, or light exercise can also ease some of the symptoms of nicotine withdrawal.

Maintaining a Smoke-Free Lifestyle

There's an old smoker's saying, "Quitting is easy. I've done it a thousand times!" Most former addicts relapse at some point before quitting for good.

Some people cave in quickly. They light up "just one last cigarette" or give in to one of their usual smoking triggers soon after quitting. Sometimes quitters who have been tobacco free for months may relapse during times of stress or depression, or maybe when they suddenly get together with old friends who smoke.

Quitters can maintain their resolve by taking advantage of any support systems available. For many people, this is the encouragement of a network of family and friends. Some smokers who quit join a smoking cessation program to share their ups and downs with a group of quitters going through the same experience. There are online resources that offer tips and support for quitters.

Staying tobacco free takes focus and persistence. It's possible to overcome a relapse—a single cigarette doesn't have to lead back to a pack-a-day habit. The quitter needs to reassert his or her willpower, analyze how to prevent another relapse, and concentrate once again on how much brighter the future looks when it isn't clouded by cigarette smoke.

Glossary

addiction The state of being dependent on something.

additive A substance, often a flavoring or preservative, that is added to products to enhance them in some manner.

cancer A malignant growth or tumor caused by abnormal and uncontrolled cell division.

carbon monoxide An odorless, flavorless gas given off as a cigarette burns that deprives red blood cells of oxygen when it is inhaled.

carcinogen A cancer-causing agent.

cardiovascular Having to do with the heart and circulatory system.

chronic bronchitis A condition in which the airways in the lungs become irritated and inflamed, and which is frequently marked by a persistent cough.

curing A method of drying freshly picked tobacco leaves so that they are more suitable for smoking.

deadly nightshade A highly poisonous plant commonly found in some parts of the United States.

emphysema A condition that occurs when the tiny air sacs inside the lungs have been damaged, making it difficult for oxygen to enter the bloodstream.

larynx The part of the throat that contains the vocal cords.

metabolism Chemical reactions that occur as the body works to sustain life, often associated with breaking down food and burning calories.

secondhand smoke The smoke from the burning end of a cigarette, as well as the smoke exhaled by smokers.

smokeless tobacco Tobacco that is taken in a form other than by smoking, most often by chewing or snorting.

stimulant An agent that stimulates or speeds up chemical reactions within the body.

stroke A blockage of blood vessels in the brain.

tar A chemically complex, dark, sticky material in cigarettes that gives them their flavor.

tolerance A condition in which the body builds a resistance to a drug, requiring the user to take more of it to achieve the desired effect.

withdrawal The process of ceasing to use an addictive drug, often accompanied by physical and emotional changes to a person's body.

For More Information

American Cancer Society

1599 Clifton Road NE

Atlanta, GA 30329-4251

(800) 227-2345

Web site: http://www.cancer.org

The American Cancer Society is an organization devoted to eliminating cancer as a major health problem through prevention and improved treatments.

American Lung Association

1740 Broadway

New York, NY 10019-4374

(800) 586-4872

Web site: http://www.lungusa.org

The American Lung Association promotes lung health with educational programs about air quality, tobacco use, emphysema, bronchitis, and chronic lung disease.

Canadian Council for Tobacco Control

75 Albert Street, Suite 508

Ottawa, ON K1P 5E7

Canada

(800) 267-5234

Web site: http://www.cctc.ca

E-mail: info-services@cctc.ca

The Canadian Council for Tobacco Control was founded by several Canadian antismoking groups. The organization focuses on ending the tobacco epidemic in Canada.

Nicotine Anonymous

P.O. Box 50177

San Francisco, CA 94159-1777

(800) 642-0666

Web site: http://www.nicotine-anonymous.org

Nicotine Anonymous is a twelve-step program offering support to those who want to quit using tobacco products.

Web Sites

Due to the changing nature of Internet links, Rosen Publishing has developed an online list of Web sites related to the subject of this book. This site is updated regularly. Please use this link to access the list:

http://www.rosenlinks.com/idd/toba

For Further Reading

Balkin, Karin, ed. *Opposing Viewpoints: Tobacco and Smoking*. Farmington Hills, MI: Greenhaven Press, 2005.

Bellenir, Karen. *Smoking Concerns Sourcebook*. Detroit, MI: Omnigraphics, 2004.

Bellenir, Karen, ed. *Tobacco Information for Teens: Health Tips About the Hazards of Using Cigarettes, Smokeless Tobacco and Other Nicotine Products*. Detroit, MI: Omnigraphics, 2006.

Connolly, Sean. *Tobacco: Just the Facts*. Portsmouth, NH: Heinemann Publishing, 2000.

Fisher, Edwin B., Jr. *7 Steps to a Smoke-Free Life*. Hoboken, NJ: John Wiley & Sons, Inc., 1998.

Heyes, Eileen. *Tobacco U.S.A.: The Industry Behind the Smoke Curtain*. Brookfield, CT: Twenty-First Century Books, 1999.

Mackay, Judith, Michael Erickson, and Omar Shafey. *The Tobacco Atlas*. Atlanta, GA: American Cancer Society, 2006.

Wagner, Heather Lehr. *Nicotine*. New York, NY: Chelsea House Publications, 2003.

Bibliography

Brizer, David. *Quitting Smoking for Dummies*. Hoboken, NJ: John Wiley & Sons, Inc., 2003.

Fisher, Edwin B., Jr. *7 Steps to a Smoke-Free Life*. Hoboken, NJ: John Wiley & Sons, Inc., 1998.

Glantz, Stanton. *The Cigarette Papers*. Berkeley, CA: University of California Press, 1996.

Hilts, Philip J. *Smokescreen: The Truth Behind the Tobacco Industry Cover-Up*. Reading, MA: Addison-Wesley Publishing Company, 1996.

Kleinman, Lowell, and Debora Messina. *The Complete Idiot's Guide to Quitting Smoking*. Indianapolis, IN: Alpha Books, 2000.

Kuhn, Cynthia. *Buzzed: The Straight Facts About the Most Used and Abused Drugs from Alcohol to Ecstasy*. New York, NY: W. W. Norton and Company, 2003.

Slovic, Paul, ed. *Smoking: Risk, Perception, and Policy*. Thousand Oaks, CA: Sage Publications, 2001.

Weil, Andrew, and Winifred Rosen. *From Chocolate to Morphine: Everything You Need to Know About Mind-Altering Drugs*. Wilmington, MA: Houghton Mifflin, 2004.

Index

About the Author

Jason Porterfield has written more than twenty books for Rosen Publishing on subjects ranging from American history to Norse mythology, as well as entries for Rosen's Teen Health and Wellness database. His books on science-related topics include *Looking at How Species Compete* and *Looking at the Human Impact on the Environment with Graphic Organizers*. He currently lives in Chicago.

Photo Credits

Cover, p. 1 © www.istockphoto.com/Maciej Laska; pp. 3, 12, 19, 31, 41, 43, 45, 46, 47 © www.istockphoto.com/Karim Hesham; pp. 7, 16, 37, 38 © Getty Images; p. 9 Courtesy Everett Collection; p. 11 © Custom Medical Stock Photo; p. 13 © www.istockphoto.com/Nathan Watkins; p. 18 © Martin Dohrn/Photo Researchers, Inc.; p. 20 © AFP/Getty Images; p. 23 © Biophoto Associates/Photo Researchers, Inc.; p. 25 © Caliendo/Custom Medical Stock Photo; p. 28 © Martin M. Rotker/Photo Researchers, Inc.; p. 29 © Jim Varney/Photo Researchers, Inc.; p. 33 © Pascal Goetgheluck/Photo Researchers, Inc.; p. 35 © Jeff Greenberg/age fotostock.

Editor: Nicholas Croce; **Designer:** Les Kanturek;
Photo Researcher: Cindy Reiman